Ransom Reading Stars

Drag Race
by Stephen Rickard

Published by Ransom Publishing Ltd.
Unit 7, Brocklands Farm, West Meon, Hampshire GU32 1JN, UK
www.ransom.co.uk

ISBN   978 178591 836 0
First published in 2010
This revised edition published 2019
Reprinted 2023

Copyright © 2019 Ransom Publishing Ltd.
Text copyright © 2019 Ransom Publishing Ltd.
All photographs copyright © 2009: inside front cover - Kev; title page - Royalbroil; countdown lights - Sam Sefton. All other photographs copyright Carter Motorsport, to whom many thanks.

A CIP catalogue record of this book is available from the British Library.

All rights reserved. No part of this publication may be reproduced, stored in a retrieval system, or transmitted, in any form or by any means, electronic, mechanical, photocopying, recording or otherwise, without the prior permission of the publishers.

The right of Stephen Rickard to be identified as the author of this Work has been asserted by him in accordance with sections 77 and 78 of the Copyright, Design and Patents Act 1988.

The Top Fuel Dragster

Wings.
Help keep the car on the track.

Fuel.
The car uses a special fuel called nitromethane. The car uses about 56 litres of fuel in a single race.

Front wheels.
All power goes to the back wheels, so the front wheels are very small and light.

Body.
Most of the body is made of carbon fibre. This makes it very light.

Engine.
The engine is about seventy times more powerful than the engine in a normal car.

Tyres.
The big tyres transfer power to the track. The tyres wear out after about 6 races.

Top Fuel Dragster Data
Length: 8.2 metres
Engine: 7,000 horse power
Top speed: 508 km/hour (317 mph)

This car is called a Top Fuel dragster. Top Fuel dragsters are the fastest cars in the world.

SECONDS
00.00

These dragsters take part in drag races. In a drag race, two dragsters race each other.

The race is only a quarter of a mile (0.4 km) long, which is not very far. There are no corners; the race is a straight line from start to finish.

ACCELERATION

BROWN TROUSERS

There's a risk that the dragster might catch fire, so I wear special clothes for the race.

I wear a full-body fire suit, with a fireproof face mask, socks and gloves. My helmet covers my face.

My helmet is also fixed to my seat, to protect my neck. The dragster goes so fast that, if my helmet wasn't fixed, I could break my neck.

Before the race, I spin the tyres to warm them up.

This is called the burnout.

SECONDS
00.00

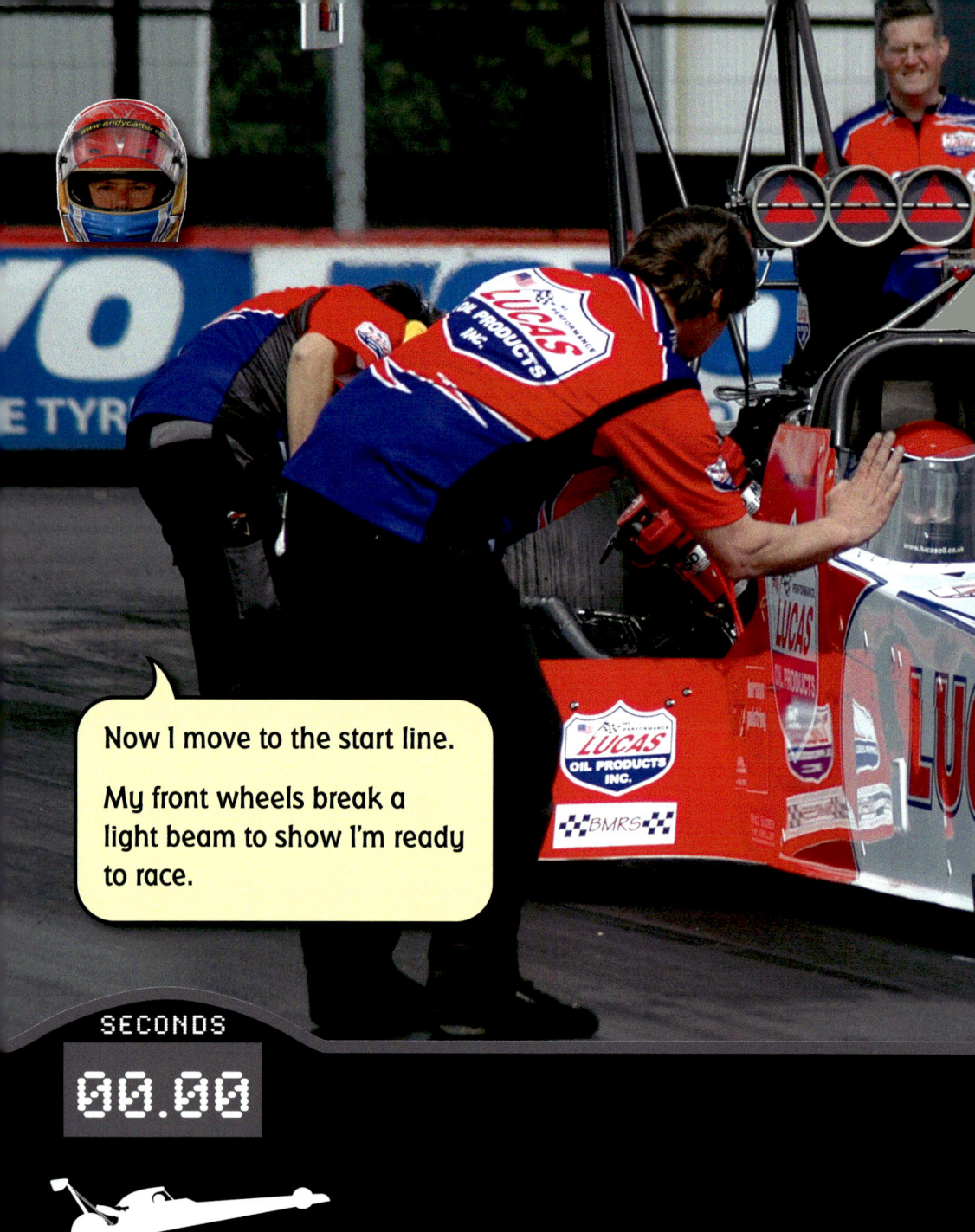

Now I move to the start line.

My front wheels break a light beam to show I'm ready to race.

SECONDS
00.00

Less than half a second later, the green lights turn on.

Go! Go! Go!

SECONDS
00.05

> My head slams back against my seat as the dragster shoots forward.
>
> The force pushing me back is as big as six people sitting on my chest. I can't move.

SECONDS
00.20

My front wheels are in the air. This is good.

It means that all the weight is pressing on the back wheels. This makes the dragster go faster.

SECONDS
01.00

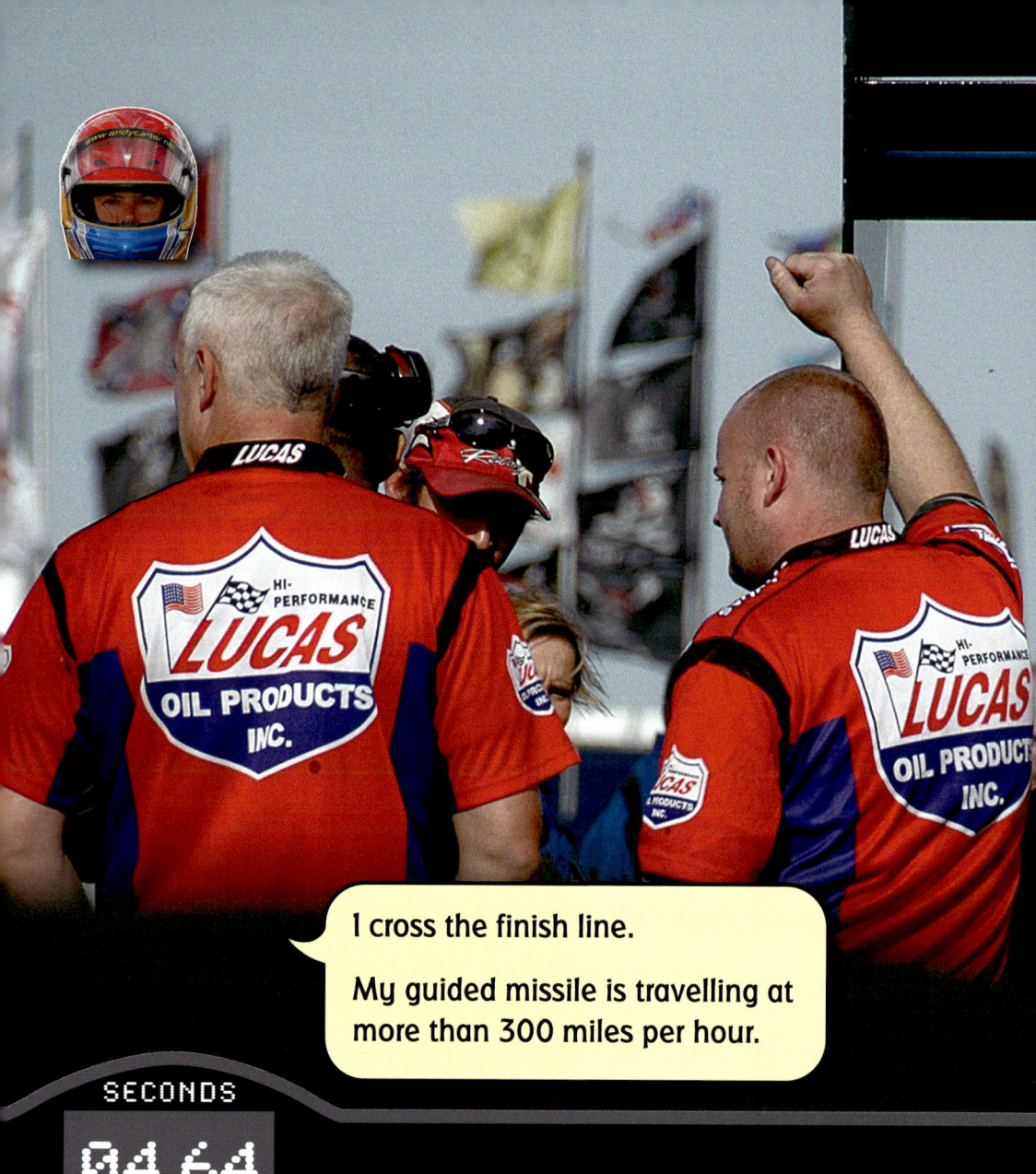

I cross the finish line.

My guided missile is travelling at more than 300 miles per hour.

SECONDS
04.64

Jargon Buster (word list)

accelerating
acceleration
burnout
carbon fibre
drag race
dragster
equivalent

fireproof
guided missile
missile
nitromethane
litre
Top Fuel dragster
tyres